Mergers and Acquisitions

The Good, The Bad and The Ugly

By Tom Charman

Introduction

The usual question that arises is: 'What is the difference between a **merger** and an acquisition (**takeover**)?' These two are commonly used together, without actually analysing whether a case could be a merger or an acquisition.

Therefore it is important to distinguish between the two. This introduction gives a brief and informative definition between the two.

A **merger** is an agreement between the management as well as shareholders of two companies, which are generally of equal size, which brings together the companies under one board of directors. Mergers are **voluntary**.

An **acquisition** is also known as a takeover. A takeover is when one company acquires the controlling stake in another company by holding 50% or more of its share capital. There are two types of takeovers. These are **friendly** and **hostile**. When a takeover is friendly, the board of directors and shareholders agrees it. When it is hostile, the shareholders or the board of directors do not agree it.

This book gives an in depth analysis of 25 large mergers and acquisitions that have taken place over the past 30 years, as well as some of the effects that it has had on the business. Therefore it is perfect for use as examples when looking for mergers and acquisitions for Business Studies at A-Level, or even to a degree level. **Tom Charman** a keen Business Studies student, as well as an entrepreneur, set up his first business at the age of 17 and has written this book to try and help students to write more broadly when constructing essays. He has a passion for business within the world around him.

Summary of Contents

According to Industry

Automotive Industry

Retail Industry

Electronic/Technological Industry

Pharmaceutical Industry

Financial Industry

Petroleum Industry

Final Conclusion

Contents of Mergers and Acquisitions

Automotive Industry

Contents of Mergers and Acquisitions

Retail Industry

Contents of Mergers and Acquisitions

Technological Industry

Contents of Mergers and Acquisitions

Pharmaceutical Industry

Contents of Mergers and Acquisitions

Financial Industry

Contents of Mergers and Acquisitions

Petroleum Industry

Automotive Industry

Daimler and Chrysler

Daimler and Chrysler

Merger Formed in:
- **May 1998**

Merger was created because:
- **Industry** became **more and more competitive**, and made it more **difficult to remain competitive**
  - Therefore merger was meant to make **them more competitive** within the market as an **'equal merger'**
  - **Greater economies of scale, shared information** and **production methods**

Daimler Paid:
- **$37bn**

General Public Response (Any Effects, i.e. Price):
- **Initially public** were in **agreement** with the **merger**
  - However as the **'equal merger' failed** to remain equal **complaints soared**
  - Public **complained** about **the unequal merger**
- **Created German and US tension**

Media Response:
- As it **was 3rd largest value merger** very **positive response**
  - **No realisation** that the **two firms** were so **different**
  - Very **high media coverage** due to the **size of merger**

Employees Response (Any Effects, i.e. Redundancies):
- **De-moralised** due to the **over-controlling parent firm**
  - As **more staff** (up to **13,000**) began to **become redundant**, the **de-moralisation continued**
- More and more staff felt **less motivated** due to **job security**, as well as the over-controlling parent firm

Any Government Intervention:
- **Approved by the Competition Commission** within Germany, and the ICC
  - **No intervention by either government**, as it did not make them market leader
    - Should have **created Economies of Scale**
  - **Merger** was **expected** to be **very successful**

Sales since acquisition:
- **Falling sales** since the merger, due to **culture clashes** between the two businesses.
  - **Democratic vs. Autocratic**, the two cultures were very contrasting
- **Since de-merger sales** have still **fallen considerably**
- **Billions** of Euros **losses** for both firms

Share Price rise or fall:
- **As merger was failing, share prices fell to below €25**
  - ○ This was just **after** the construction of **the Eurozone**
- Share price for **March 2012**, currently **sits at €47.18 per share**
  - ○ Considerably **higher** that it was **14 years** ago
- However, **since de-merger**, and the recovery of Daimler, **share price** has been sitting at a **steady rate**
- **Chrysler** was **bought by Fiat in 2011**
  - ○ Therefore the **share price** of Chrysler was particularly **low**, but now it has **improved significantly** since the **acquisition by Fiat**

What the merger has meant for Daimler/Chrysler:
- **Huge losses** within the firm
- Led to **de-merger** of the two companies
- Losses led to **falling productivity**
  - ○ High **unemployment** and **bad publicity**

Any Problems within the business:
- Eventually **led to de-merger**
  - ○ This was due to **corporate culture clashes**

Short-term effects:
- **Integration issues** during transitional period
- **Staff morale falling** as parent firm very controlling

Long-term effects:
- In **2000, the business suffered third quarter losses** of more than **half a billion dollars**
  - ○ **Projections** of even **higher losses** in the fourth quarter and into **2001**
- In early 2001, the **merged company** announced that it would **slash 26,000 jobs** at its failing **Chrysler division**

References

http://news.bbc.co.uk/1/hi/business/88912.stm

http://abcnews.go.com/WNT/story?id=131280&page=1#.T2YxE5j7XoA

http://www.casestudyinc.com/daimler-chrysler-and-the-failed-merger

http://www.streetdirectory.com/travel_guide/53007/car_focus/how_daimler_chrysler_merger_failed.html

http://www.autocar.co.uk/www.autocar.co.uk/News/NewsArticle/AllCars/257504/

http://www.lordofthewebs.com/communication/dailmlerChrysler.pdf

http://www.businessweek.com/2000/00_23/b3684147.htm

ord and Jaguar Land Rover

Ford and Jaguar Land Rover (JLR)

Merger Formed in:
- **December 1989**

Merger was created because:
- To **compete** with other **international** car manufacturers
  - The merger would allow Ford **to target new markets** with new consumers
- The move **to introduce Land Rover** and **Jaguar** into **America** should see sales rise considerably
- Also **to share information** and production methods
  - Could allow Ford to create their own all-wheel drive models

Ford Paid:
- **$2.5bn**
  - **5 time the value worth** of Jaguar
- Later bought Land Rover

General Public Response (Any Effects, i.e. Price):
- **General public** felt that it was a **move away** from the **traditional brand** and could create problems
  - Later realized that the model that Ford created, the **'baby Jag'** was a complete **disaster**
- Felt **that Ford** would change the **culture of Jaguar and Land Rover**

Media Response:
- Media was **sceptical** that JLR would **lose** all of its **'British tradition'**
  - The media felt that **once Ford owned JLR** it would be **entirely taken over** and the traditional cars removed
    - Ford would simply focus on producing the **large all-wheel drive models** for **high returns** on their **investment**

Any Government Intervention:
- **No government intervention**, as it was felt that **other businesses** had much **larger market share** within the **automotive industry**
  - Therefore it was **not considered anti-competitive**
- There were **concerns** about how many **job redundancies** were **expected**
  - Government tried **to prevent as may job redundancies** as possible
- There were a **large number of mergers** in the **industry (GM and Fiat)**

Employees Response (Any Effects, i.e. Redundancies):
- **Some redundancies necessary** as overlap between two **companies**
  - Therefore **some job dissatisfaction** and **a fall in job security**
- However the business did **not** face much **revolt** from staff

Sales since acquisition:
- **Sales grew initially** when the **business integrated**
  - However after **targeting the wrong market, sales** fell and **reputation fell**
- Ford was later **force to sell** to **Tata**, due to huge losses

Share Price rise or fall:
- The share price **just before** the merger in 1989 saw **share price rise**
  - ○ Even though the buyout was much higher than the value
- Therefore this **meant investors** had **confidence**
- However **share price fell rapidly** for Ford **until** the **sale** of the company to Tata

What the merger meant for Ford/JLR:
- The **ability** to **share information**
  - ○ **Possibility** to become **more productive** under **one leadership** style
- However there was a **problem with fully integrating** the business which meant that sales did not actually grow to forecast
  - ○ This eventually **led to the failure** of the merger due to poor sales

Any Problems within the business:
- **Failure** to **predict** the **markets**
- Ford released a Jaguar that was against the general opinion of public
  - ○ The **'baby Jag' was deemed a complete failure** by the media
- **Corporate culture** clashes meant that it was **difficult to fully integrate** the business
  - ○ Led to a **failure in the merger**

Short-term effects:
- **Higher share price**
  - ○ Although it was considered that Ford paid too much, **Jaguar was still** seen as a **growing company** that could give **high returns**
- There were **some integration costs**

Long-term effects:
- The **ability to fully integrate** the business was **unsuccessful**, which meant that there were **high costs**
  - ○ **Marketing was poor**, and Ford was targeting the wrong market due to their **inexperience**
- **Corporate culture clashes** between the two business, while one was focused on **quality** and one was focused on **mass production**
- Eventually led to the **de-merger** and sale of **JLR to Tata**

References:

http://www.nytimes.com/1990/03/22/business/company-news-ford-paid-jaguar-2-hillion-premium.html

http://www.drive.com.au/editorial/articledetail.aspx?ArticleID=1406&vf=1

http://www.ehow.com/facts_5181186_jaguar-car-history.html

http://www.fundinguniverse.com/company-histories/Ford-Motor-Company-Company-History.html

http://en.wikipedia.org/wiki/Ford_Motor_Company

ata and Jaguar Land Rover

Tata and Jaguar Land Rover (JLR)

Merger Formed in:
- **June 2008**

Merger was created because:
- Tata wanted **presence outside India**
  - ○ They wanted to **diversify their product range**
- Could take advantage of **low cost manufacturing**
  - ○ Ford were selling it **cheaply** due to the problems they faced

Tata Paid:
- **$2.3bn**

General Public Response (Any Effects, i.e. Price):
- Tata was an **international competitor**
  - ○ Therefore **public feared job cuts** to move production to cheaper country
- However consumers believed that it could **not get worse after Ford** so welcomed merger
- **Other car manufactures** also **welcomed** Tata and its JLR acquisition **with 'open arms'**

Media Response:
- **Positive** of the merger
  - ○ Felt that the merger between **Ford and JLR was a failure**
    - ▪ Therefore hoped that **Tata** would be **successful** at doing it better
  - ○ Therefore felt it was the **best move for consumers**

Any Government Intervention:
- **Cleared** by the **UKCC** as well as **international bodies**
  - ○ Was **not deemed anti-competitive** as Tata were moving into a **new market**
    - ▪ Therefore they did **not** have a **large market share in luxury car market**
    - ▪ Allowed them therefore to buy JLR

Employees Response (Any Effects, i.e. Redundancies):
- After merger most **staff remained** and **were integrated into Tata**
  - ○ However Tata **moved towards closing plants of production** in UK
  - ○ Therefore **staff losses were inevitable**
- **Some redundancies** were made, however **not huge numbers**
  - ○ Tata is now looking towards **integrating Jaguar and Land Rover plants**

Sales since acquisition:
- After Ford sold JLR to Tata sales begin to **rise**
  - ○ **Ford failed to integrate** JLR into the business
- Tata **successfully bought the firm** by running JLR separately
  - ○ This allowed JLR to **continue to function** and **sales** begin to **rise** dramatically
    - ▪ Now sales continue to grow not just in developed economies but also developing economies such as China and more middle class countries

Share Price rise or fall:
- Immediately after merger, **share price fell** dramatically to a **4 cent share** value
  - ○ However since this, and as **JLR is now performing strongly**, share price has risen higher and higher to a **price today of 26 cents.**
    - ▪ Therefore the merger was **successful in the eyes of investors**

What the merger meant for Tata/JLR:
- Pushed **Tata into the higher market share of the market**
  - ○ Meant that they were **operating outside India**, and **had presence across the globe**
- The **high market share** would probably **lead to high profits**
  - ○ They could **exploit different markets** and consumers

Any Problems within the business:
- Moved into a **very volatile market**
  - ○ Many were **sceptical about how successful Tata** could operate
- **Required large funding** including **bridge loans** that threatened the strength of the business
  - ○ Therefore meant that the **long-term success could not be guaranteed**
- Employee **pay within Tata** became more **unstable and volatile**

Short-term effects:
- **Integration costs** and trying to improve reputation after Ford
  - ○ Costs involved in **innovation (bridge loans)**
- Moves towards **international production**, and therefore **redundancy costs**

Long-term effects:
- **Revival of JLR and its profitability**
  - ○ Tata **successfully turned JLR** around and made it **profitable**
- Therefore Tata **gained higher profits** and market share within luxury car market
  - ○ **JLR became more profitable** which meant the merger was not only a friendly merger but also a **success at bringing the two firms together**
    - ▪ Tata **invested heavily into JLR innovation and employees**

References:

http://www.oppapers.com/essays/Tata-Jaguar-Merging/373295

http://www.slideshare.net/Lordnikhil/tata-jlr-acquisition-case-study

http://www.scribd.com/doc/40310575/Merger-Acquistion-Process-in-India-With-JLR-TATA-Merger-Case-Study

http://www.google.co.uk/finance?client=ob&q=NYSE:TTM

http://www.financialexpress.com/news/tata-motors-completes-jlr-acquisition/317619/

http://www.tata.com/media/releases/inside.aspx?artid=mCgnlgckTZw

Retail Industry

Kraft and Cadburys

Kraft and Cadburys

Merger Formed in:
- **February 2010**

Merger was created because:
- To Create **economies of scale**
- To move into **emerging markets**
- **Knowledge sharing**
- Become much more involved in **confectionary in Europe**

Kraft Paid:
- **£11.5bn ($19.6bn)**

General Public Response (Any Effects, i.e. Price):
- **Kraft** recently **raised the price of products**, however **claims** this is **due to inflation**
- Have not been affected severely since takeover and the 'Olympics' **campaign by Cadburys** has meant that there is **large investment** into the **company by Kraft**

Media Response:
- **Negative response by media**, saying that Kraft would axe jobs, and that it was not the best decision for Cadburys
- May not be feasible in the long run, and still float concerns about the company

Employees Response (Any Effects, i.e. Redundancies):
- **150 Job Cuts**
    - Many problems with employees at factory in short run
    - Led to **strikes** which did in the short run **effect production levels**
    - However, after merger, the company now accounts for having **50 of its executive staff from Cadburys**, and therefore there were not huge redundancies

Any Government Intervention:
- No further job cuts by Kraft agreed with MP's in the UK
- Although no formal intervention by government, 'strong concerns' still at large within the house and business committee, and will intervene if necessary

Sales since acquisition:
- **Sales have risen by 30%** for Kraft since merger
    - However, profits have fallen due to the costs that Cadburys causes to the company due to the ingredients, and to some extent rising prices of cocoa beans
    - **Net Profit down 24% in fourth quarter 2010** (£335m due to integration of business)

Share Price rise or fall:
- Share price has been rising since the takeover of Cadburys by Kraft
    - **$26.70 a share up to $38.30 a share to 2012**

What the merger has meant for Kraft/Cadburys:
- **Higher Profits**
- **Higher share price** and therefore **greater investment**

Any Problems within the business:
- Still analysed heavily by the government of the UK
- No further job cuts
- However, share price rising, and profits now rising

Short-term effects:
- **Strikes** and protest by **factory staff**
- **Integration costs** of **£335m** affecting profits

Long-term effects:
- **Greater economies of scale** for the merged company, leading to **greater profits**
- Greater **expansion** into larger and more **diverse markets**

References:

http://www.slideshare.net/HenriMoufettal/ma-kraft-cadbury

http://uk.finance.yahoo.com/echarts?s=KFT#symbol=kft;range=5y;compare=;indicator=volume;chart type=area;crosshair=on;ohlcvalues=0;logscale=off;source=undefined;

http://news.bbc.co.uk/1/hi/8467007.stm

http://www.bbc.co.uk/news/business-12427830

http://www.ft.com/cms/s/0/71a34530-2019-11e0-a6fb-00144feab49a.html#axzz1pHAoU6yp

http://www.telegraph.co.uk/finance/newsbysector/epic/cbry/

Co-op and Somerfield

Co-Operative Foods and Somerfield

Merger Formed in:
- **January 2009**

Merger was created because:
- Co-op sought to **increase its market share** within the highly competitive supermarket chains and therefore bought **Somerfield with 3.6% market** share to increase **Co-op to the 5th largest** chain

Co-op Paid:
- **£1.6bn**

General Public Response (Any Effects, i.e. Price):
- Large number of general public **complaining** about the 'staff attitudes' and 'swearing, overcharging** and **food safety concerns'**

Media Response:
- **Positive**, arguing it is **good for the UK economy**
  - ○ **Greater economies of scale** can be achieved
  - ○ Company is not huge, but things such as **'Take on Tesco'**

Employees Response (Any Effects, i.e. Redundancies):
- **Staff morale** has **fallen considerably** since the merger between Somerfield and Co-op
- **Redundancies of over 750**, since the **closing** of the **HQ of Somerfield's**
- Still **integration problems** regarding the **two companies**, with **further redundancies likely**

Any Government Intervention:
- Due to the **size** of the two stores Co-op and Somerfield (**4.1% and 3.6%** respectively), **no intervention** required by the government
- **OFT agreed merger** between two **companies in late 2008**
- Although some redundancies, does **not threaten UK market**, so no great problems regarding government. **Both UK firms**

Sales since acquisition:
- Sales **fallen by 3.38% LFL sales** for the **Somerfield sales** while there has been a **rise** by **0.13% LFL sales**

Share Price rise or fall:
- **129.5 per share before acquisition**
  - ○ **Fell considerably** since global **economic downturn**
    - ■ Now recovering, therefore **share price** is at **125.75**, however did slump to a low of **114 in 2011**

What the merger has meant for Co-op/Somerfield:
- **Higher profits**, since merger, of **around 20% LFL** by **final quarter of 2010**
- **Greater market share** within a very **highly competitive market**

Any Problems within the business:
- **Poor customer service** issues possibly due to **motivational issues**
- The **sales** for Somerfield stores is **now falling**, while Co-op continues to benefit
- **Problems** with completing the **integration of the merger**

Short-term effects:
- **Integration issues**, during the **transitional period** between integrating Somerfield into Co-op
- **Problems** with **customer knowledge**, leading to issues regarding **sales and complaints**

Long-term effects:
- **Higher sales** due to higher market share
- **Greater presence** within the market
  - ○ Customers more aware of the Co-op brand
- **Higher profitability** due to the greater number of stores
- **Greater economies of scale**
- **Lower unit cost**

References:

http://www.co-operative.coop/corporate/aboutus/Somerfield/Somerfield/Somerfield-History/

http://www.independent.co.uk/news/business/news/coop-struggles-continue-with-somerfield-takeover-7447375.html

http://www.independent.co.uk/news/business/news/coop-to-shut-somerfield-hq-after-takeover-1623407.html

http://news.sky.com/home/business/article/15576064

http://en.wikipedia.org/wiki/Somerfield

Quaker and Snapple

Quaker and Snapple

Merger Formed in:
- **November 1994**

Merger was created because:
- **The success of Gatorade**, made Quaker want to **'snap up' Snapple** before any of their competitors could, and **introduce** the successful **label** into every **supermarket chain** and **store** that they **could**

Quaker Paid:
- **$1.7bn**

General Public Response (Any Effects, i.e. Price):
- **Public liked** the **brand**, however when bought by Quaker, sales began to fall
  - Quaker **failed to realise customer market**
    - **Branded product wrong**
  - Therefore there were **complaints** about the merger

Media Response:
- Wall street argued that it was **likely to fail**
  - Argued that they **paid too much**
  - Argued they **jumped** on the 'band wagon' **too quickly**
- **Later branded** as the **'biggest flop'** regarding mergers and acquisitions

Employees Response (Any Effects, i.e. Redundancies):
- **Staff motivation fell**, due to constant **movement** between **firms**
  - Felt **demotivated** as they were being **'taken for a ride'**
- **Staff redundancies** also affected motivation due to **job security**

Any Government Intervention:
- **No government intervention**
  - Agreement by US Competition Commission
- Made them 3rd largest beverage company in North America

Sales since acquisition:
- Sales **fell considerably** due to **failure to realise market**, and approach taken by Snapple
- Led to a huge loss in Quaker, as marketing campaign cost millions but sales fell

Share Price rise or fall:
- **Quaker's stock sank $7.375**, or almost **10 percent**, to **$67.125 a share** on the New York Stock Exchange. **Snapple shares fell 50 cents**, to **$13.75**, in heavy Nasdaq trading, and angry **Snapple shareholders** raced to the courthouse to **block** what they viewed as a **distasteful bid**.
- **Constant falling share prices** since purchase **until sale to Triarc**

What the merger has meant for Quaker/Snapple:
- **De-merger** of the company **to the company Triarc**, however it **also tarnished CEO of Quaker** and led to his removal
- Also meant that **Quaker lost considerable support and face poor publicity**

Any Problems within the business:
- **Quaker did not realise** the marketing success Snapple had from **targeting small independent stores**
  - ○ Therefore **after** the merger, the **sales began to fall**, and the **marketing campaign** was branded a **complete failure**

Short-term effects:
- In the **short term**, huge **spending** on a marketing campaign **to introduce Snapple into supermarkets**
- **Integration costs** after purchase by Quaker of Snapple

Long-term effects:
- Ended up **selling Snapple to Triarc for $300m**, making a **huge loss** on their initial purchase of **$1.7bn**
- **Falling sales**, due to **poor branding** and **poor customer awareness**
- Failure to carry out the product, **led to failure of the merger**

References:

http://money.ca.msn.com/savings-debt/gallery/gallery.aspx?cp-documentid=23482925&page=4

http://www.rasmussen.edu/degrees/business/blog/best-and-worst-corporate-mergers/

http://www.nytimes.com/1994/11/03/business/company-reports-quaker-oats-to-acquire-snapple.html?pagewanted=all&src=pm

http://articles.latimes.com/1997-03-28/business/fi-42931_1_quaker-bought-snapple

http://www.nytimes.com/1997/03/28/business/quaker-to-sell-snapple-for-300-million.html?pagewanted=all&src=pm

http://www.ftc.gov/be/rt/businesreviewpaper.pdf

L'Oreal and The Body Shop

L'Oreal and The Body Shop

Merger Formed in:
- **March 2006**

Merger was created because:
- The **large market share** The Body Shop holds, would **compliment** the **L'Oreal products** that they own
  - Therefore they **sought to buy The Body Shop** due to the benefits of **greater market share** and the **complimentary products** it supplies
    - The **Body Shop has 2085 stores worldwide**

L'Oreal Paid:
- **£652m**

General Public Response (Any Effects, i.e. Price):
- **Popularity fell immediately** after L'Oreal bought The Body Shop
- This was due to the **ethics** that **involved The Body Shop**
  - L'Oreal **not so ethical compared** with **The Body Shop**

Media Response:
- **Mixed response**, with some agreeing it as a positive
- Some regarded the merger as a bad idea due to the **ethics** involved
  - **The ethics issue** is what regularly **arose** with both the **general public and the media**

Employees Response (Any Effects, i.e. Redundancies):
- **No great issues**, as there were **no plans to create redundancies**
  - Intended to keep **model the same** however, L'Oreal would gain profits
- **Only issue** was the issue **regarding ethics**
  - The **UK** stores also had **some reservations** as The Body Shop was **initially a UK firm** that started in Brighton (Roddick was the creator)

Any Government Intervention:
- **No Government intervention** when it was acquired by L'Oreal
  - However **some moves to prevent any job redundancies**

Sales since acquisition:
- **Underperformance** since the acquisition by L'Oreal
- **Possibly due to the ethics issue**
  - The Body Shop has seen a **4.1% decline** in sales **since acquisition** by L'Oreal in 2006
- Therefore **sales have fallen**, however **argued** that this is **due to recession**

Share Price rise or fall:
- **62.8p per share** up to **98.75p per share** since acquisition by L'Oreal up until December 2007
- However L'Oreal saw a **crisis in 2008** that saw share **price plummet** to a **low of 50.19 per share**
  - Now been **recovering** and moving at **a steady upwards rate** since this plummet

What the merger meant for L'Oreal/The Body Shop:
- **Greater profitability** for L'Oreal, as they were a **very similar company** within the same market
- **L'Oreal had a greater market** share due to the **stores worldwide** that The Body Shop held
- **Greater markets** due to **broad range of countries** that The Body Shop operates within

Any Problems within the business:
- **Ethics for the business**
  - The **Body Shop** was considering to be **moving away** from its **ethical products** due to L'Oreal's **testing on animals**
- The Body Shop did **not have such high returns as expected**

Short-term effects:
- **Creating the positive image**, due to the **publicity** of **poor ethics**
- **Integration issues** into the **business**
- **Corporate culture differences**

Long-term effects:
- Likely **greater sales** in the long run leading to **greater profitability**
- **Wider markets** for **L'Oreal to exploit**
- **Product information** and **divergence between the two businesses**
  - Allows for **greater Economies of Scale** and new **innovation**

References:

http://news.bbc.co.uk/1/hi/4815776.stm

http://www.independent.co.uk/news/uk/this-britain/body-shops-popularity-plunges-after-loreal-sale-473599.html

http://www.cosmeticsdesign-europe.com/Business-Financial/L-Oreal-s-Body-Shop-acquisition-meets-with-mixed-reaction

http://www.bloomberg.com/news/2011-12-12/body-shop-fails-to-return-1-billion-to-06-shareholders-retail.html

Sears and Kmart

Sears and Kmart

Merger Formed in:
- **January 2005**

Merger was created because:
- Both **retailers** were finding it **difficult to keep up** with the **changes** in **American retail**
  - ○ Therefore this **merger** would **create the 3rd largest retailer** in the country
- Should make them **more competitive** against **companies** such as **Wall-Mart and Target**
- Could also **increase profitability** for the new business Sears Holdings

Kmart Paid:
- **$11bn**

General Public Response (Any Effects, i.e. Price):
- The merger would **allow the two businesses to stock similar products**
  - ○ Therefore the **consumer** may be able to **purchase the products** more **easily** due to a **greater number** of **stocked stores**
- The **price** may also **fall** due to Kmart and Sears trying to **compete against other retailers**

Media Response:
- The **media response** was **generally positive** of the merger
  - ○ **Believed it would increase** the **strength** of the **weak** but **traditional businesses**
- Therefore they **felt that the merger** would be **good** as it **might prevent** the **two traditional** and well **established businesses** from **falling into liquidation**

Any Government Intervention:
- **No government intervention** and was **agreed by competition commissions** partly due to its long term **establishment** within the **US**
  - ○ However, as well as this there are **still businesses** within retail that are **larger than Sears Holdings**, and thus there was **no anti-competitive reason** to prevent the **merger**

Employees Response (Any Effects, i.e. Redundancies):
- **The job opportunities have reduced significantly** with the **market share** of Sears Holdings **falling significantly**
  - ○ While there has been **some profitability** for the **business**, it has **lost market** share to the **competitors** such as **Target and Wall-Mart**
- **100 stores were closed** after the business received a **profit warning**

Sales since acquisition:
- Although the **merger appeared** to be **successful sales continued to fall** for the two businesses
  - ○ While **Wall-Mart and other competitors saw rising sales**, Sears Holdings sales **fell 10% between 2005 and 2009**
- Therefore the merger was **not so successful** as it led to **falling sales for both businesses**

Share Price rise or fall:
- When the **merger was announced,** Wall Street **investors applauded the deal**
  - Share price for **Kmart jumped 16%**
  - Share price for **Sears jumped $7.79, a 22% increase**
- However after the **merger continued, sales started** to **fall,** and therefore **share price also fell** considerably
  - Share price for Sears Holdings is **$69.66 per share**
    - Although this **has increased,** the share price is **beginning** to **fall considerably**

What the merger meant for Kmart/Sears:
- It **should have increased profitability** and allowed for a greater market share, as the business would become the **3rd largest retail business** behind Wall-Mart
  - However the merger actually led to **continued falling sales** for both businesses, which has **seen profits fall** and **market share decrease**

Any Problems within the business:
- Although the **website is seen as successful,** there has still **not been rising sales**
  - Customers felt **more inclined to shop at competitors such as Wall-Mart**
- Therefore the **sales were not being made up** after the merger
  - The two faced **two different problems,** and the **merger** seemed to **accentuate** the **problems** for each business

Short-term effects:
- There were **integration costs** and **unsurprising redundancies**
  - However should also **mean that profits can increase** in the long run due to cost **savings and no overlap**

Long-term effects:
- There has **been falling sales** and **therefore falling profits**
  - This has led to **falling profitability** and **market share** which has **damaged the reputation** of the business
- Investors as well as Sears Holdings **claim falling sales** due to the **great recession,** however **competitors** within the market have **continued to grow,** and **therefore take market share** from Sears Holdings
- Although **profitable,** the growth of the **business has almost stopped,** with the risk of it **falling into recession** and making **losses**

References:

http://money.cnn.com/2004/11/17/news/fortune500/sears_kmart/

http://www.nytimes.com/2010/12/22/business/22sears.html?pagewanted=all

http://www.huffingtonpost.com/2011/12/27/sears-kmart-stores-closing_n_1170772.html

http://quotes.wsj.com/SHLD/interactive-chart#P5Y

http://en.wikipedia.org/wiki/Sears_Holdings_Corporation

http://www.cbsnews.com/8301-505145_162-57348594/sears-to-close-100-to-120-kmart-sears-stores/

Mattel and The Learning Company

Mattel and The Learning Company

Merger Formed in:
- **January 1995**

Merger was created because:
- **To increase market share** and **combine the different abilities** of each business
  - Seek to **exploit the two businesses** to **increase internet presence** and **increase sales**
- To **enter the educational toy market** through the established Learning Company

Mattel Paid:
- **$3.8bn**

General Public Response (Any Effects, i.e. Price):
- The **general public welcomed the merger**, due to the **educational child programs** that TLC and Mattel intended to release
  - Therefore the **educative toys seemed to be a hit** with the public which is why the public welcomed the merger

Media Response:
- The **media took a positive view** of **Mattel's decision to merge with TLC**
  - They felt it **would benefit consumers**, especially as they were looking to develop a more **educational product** and **purpose**
- Therefore the media had a **strong positive response** to **the merger** and felt it would likely succeed

Any Government Intervention:
- There was **no government intervention**, as although Mattel and TLC were dominant in countries across the world, they were **not considerably large against** other **competitors**
  - Therefore it was **felt that the merger** would **not** create any **anti-competitive** behaviour
- This led the **merger to be approved** by the **competition commission**

Employees Response (Any Effects, i.e. Redundancies):
- The **employees welcomed the merger** at first, as they believed it would be a **new way** to grow into **new markets**
  - Therefore they **believed that sales** should **rise and continue to grow**, and see the **profitability of Mattel grow**
- However as **sales fell and profitability shrunk**, along with **market share**, employees began to turn against TLC

Sales since acquisition:
- Since **acquisition sales fell** and **costs rose**
  - In less than a year **TLC lost $206m**, destroying profits for Mattel
- By **2000, Mattel was losing $1.5m** per day
  - Therefore **not only did sales fall**, but **TLC destroyed profits** for Mattel

Share Price rise or fall:
- The **share price for both immediately** after the merger **fell**
  - The **merger led to falling sales** for a number of reasons, but most of the fall was blamed on the fact that **investors were not particularly happy** about the merger between the two
- As **profits continued to fall, so did** the **share price**
  - Therefore **until the de-merger in 2000, the** profits continued to take a hit. However once the **de-merger** was **announced, share price for Mattel grew 0.44%**

What the merger meant for Mattel/The Learning Company:
- **Should have allowed Mattel to exploit the educative toy market** however did instead see **falling profits**
  - Therefore it saw **falling sales and falling profits**
- Eventually **cost Mattel so much** that they were looking to **sell it only a year after the merger** was completed

Any Problems within the business:
- There were **huge problems with integration** when the two first came together which never fully allowed them to become integrated
- There were **huge losses of $206m** after the first year, which meant that the profits for Mattel were hit very heavily by **the merger of TLC**
  - Therefore the **merger caused significant financial problems** within the company

Short-term effects:
- **Integration costs**, and problems integrating the two together
  - Therefore the **business was overall facing profit problems**, as it became difficult to **integrate the two together**
- Employees were **also made redundant** so there were some **redundancy costs involved**

Long-term effects:
- There were **huge profit problems** within one year after the merger which saw Mattel ending on a **loss of $86m** after the **$206m loss of TLC**
  - Therefore **the long term effect was a considerable loss** in profit
- This did **eventually lead to a de-merger** due to problems regarding sales and integration
- Also **damaged the reputation of the business**

References:

http://www.zdnet.com/news/mattelthe-learning-co-in-38b-merger/101179

http://www.cnbc.com/id/34467713/Top_10_Best_and_Worst_Mergers_of_All_Time?slide=9

http://www.forbes.com/2000/04/03/mu5.html

http://investor.shareholder.com/mattel/secfiling.cfm?filingID=898430-99-2991

http://en.wikipedia.org/wiki/Mattel

http://en.wikipedia.org/wiki/The_Learning_Company

Adidas and Reebok

Adidas and Reebok

Merger Formed in:
- **January 2006**

Merger was created because:
- To become **more competitive against** Nike, the **market leader** for sporting goods
  - ○ **Reebok** and **Adidas** were the **2nd and 3rd largest** and therefore would be **able to create much greater competition** by merging
- Would **close the gap** between Nike and other sporting companies
  - ○ Therefore **reduce Nike's market powers**
- Further **growth** and **profitability**, as well as **stability**

Adidas Paid:
- **$3.78bn**

General Public Response (Any Effects, i.e. Price):
- **Positive response** as it would **close the gap** between Nike and Adidas-Reebok
  - ○ Therefore Nike **may not set such high prices** which due to increase **competition**
- The **public benefits** due to **the higher level of competition** and **likely lower price** by Adidas as well as Nike

Media Response:
- The **media welcomed the merger** and believed that the **two would work well together**
  - ○ Therefore they felt that the **merger would be a positive move** towards making the sporting industry **more competitive** and benefitting consumers
- There would also be **higher profits**
  - ○ However they were **sceptical about the corporate culture clashes**

Any Government Intervention:
- The **EU Competition Commission** agreed the **merger between Adidas and Reebok**
  - ○ It was **argued** that there was **some overlap**, however they had **different pricing strategies** and therefore the merger would **not be anti-competitive** and disadvantage consumers
- It would also likely **increase competition** against Nike, the market leader for sporting goods
- **US Competition Commission** also gave the **green light** for the acquisition

Employees Response (Any Effects, i.e. Redundancies):
- The **company intended to save $120m per year** for **3 years** and thus **redundancies** were to be **expected**
  - ○ There would be **some overlap** and therefore staff would be made redundant as cost saving measures
- However, it would **also increase job security**, as the **business becomes** much **larger** and much **more competitive**
  - ○ It also **offers future opportunity** for staff within Adidas

Sales since acquisition:
- **Since the merger, sales** have continued to **rise** and become more positive for the business
  - ○ **Reebok has continued to succeed well** under **Adidas** and the two have seen growth
    - ▪ They are also **becoming much more competitive**, increasing market share

Share Price rise or fall:
- After **announcement of the merger**, both businesses saw **a rise in the share price** of the business
  - ○ **Share price for Reebok** lifted **by $13.19 to $57.14 (30%)**
  - ○ **Share price for Adidas** lifted **by 7% to $192.76 per share**
- Therefore **investors felt** that the **view to merge** the two together to form one large platform was a **positive step** to becoming **more competitive** against **the likes of Nike and Puma**

What the merger meant for Adidas/Reebok:
- The **merger allowed the business** to become much **more competitive** against its **rivals**
  - ○ Therefore they would be **able to increase the profitability** as well as sales in the **long run**
- It meant that **overall the market** became much **more competitive** that it currently is, as Nike is currently much larger

Any Problems within the business:
- There were **different cultures and goals** for each business
  - ○ While **Reebok focussed on lifestyle, Adidas focussed on sport**
- Therefore this **did initially create some issue**, however it was quickly resolved as the **new business incorporated both**

Short-term effects:
- **Some integration costs**
  - ○ Aiming at **saving $120m** a year for 3 years so **strategies also had to be laid out**
- There were **some overlaps**, so **profitability short term may have been affected**

Long-term effects:
- **Much greater profitability and ability to grow**
  - ○ The **two would work together** to become **much more competitive** and much **larger**
- There would be an **overlap in innovation**, making it **possible to become more innovative**
- There would **likely be economies of scale** that could be **benefitted** from as the two **both produce very similar items**

References:

http://www.pbleepd.com/business/top-10-business-mergersacquisitions-of-the-decade-part-2/

http://www.businessweek.com/bwdaily/dnflash/aug2005/nf20050084_8340.htm

http://www.dw.de/dw/article/0,,1870303,00.html

http://www.usatoday.com/money/industries/manufacturing/2005-08-04-adidas-1b-cover-usat_x.htm

http://timesofindia.indiatimes.com/business/india-business/Top-level-changes-at-Adidas-India/articleshow/12421414.cms

http://www.slideshare.net/shravan.bhumkar/adidas-case-study

hompsons and First Choice

Thompsons and First Choice

Merger Formed in:
- **June 2007**

Merger was created because:
- To **increase market share** within the **European Travel Market**
- To **introduce cost cutting measures increasing profitability** of the **two businesses**
  - Also **intend to increase the growth** of the internet markets

Thompsons Paid:
- The **merger was valued at £12bn**
  - **51% owned by TUI** (owners of Thompsons) and **49% First Choice**

General Public Response (Any Effects, i.e. Price):
- **TUI is the largest UK tour operator** and therefore it was **partially welcomed** by the general public
  - They believed it **may allow them to increase their presence** within the market and therefor **make it more competitive** pushing **down the price**
- Therefore **the public intended to agree**, as they believed it would **promote competition**

Media Response:
- The **media gave a generally positive view** of the merger
  - Thompsons would **continue to remain the largest tour operator** within the UK, and it would **allow them to become more competitive** within the EU
- Therefore the **media generally agreed** with the merger and believed it would help to **stimulate growth** within the UK and make it **more affordable to travel**

Any Government Intervention:
- **The UKCC agreed the merger** after consultation and agreed that the merger would not lead TUI to become anti-competitive, or indeed gain an anti-competitive advantage
  - **Therefore the go-ahead** was given to **TUI to purchase First Choice**
- However the **agreement did contain a clause** requiring TUI to **sell the Irish Budget airline**, as it would give **them too much market power** within the **Irish market**

Employees Response (Any Effects, i.e. Redundancies):
- **Employees were concerned** about the **number of job losses** that were to be **expected due to the merger**
  - Therefore there was **some concern raised** within unions that staff numbers would **drop rapidly**
- Some issues **over production did occur** due to this, as there was some **moves towards strike action** to prevent a large number of job declines

Sales since acquisition:
- **Since the acquisition of First Choice** sales have **continued to rise**
  - As the **recession hit**, the **number of people using Thompsons** airways **declined**
- However, **First Choice is a cheaper tour operator** and therefore their **sales rose**, which later proved that the **merger was successful** as it allowed for Thompsons to **exploit budget operators further**
  - TUI and First Choice **announced record profits over the 2011 trading period**

Share Price rise or fall:
- Since the **announcement of the acquisition, shares surged 27p to 311p** which was almost **10% increase share price**
  - **Therefore investors** in **First Choice** were in **agreement** with the decision to combine TUI with First Choice

What the merger meant for Thompsons/First Choice:
- The **merger allowed the businesses** to become more **competitive within the UK** but also the **EU**
  - They could both **gain from large economies of scale** regarding fuel, as well as being able to **offer different routes** and therefore **make a larger number of sales**
- It allowed them to **become more competitive internationally**
  - **Profitability would also increase** considerably **thanks to the merger** and the **combined revenue** of the two businesses

Any Problems within the business:
- The **two had some overlap** that had to be removed before the merger could run successfully together, and therefore this had to be resolved
  - This **did take around 2 months to complete**, and therefore there were some issues regarding sales and profitability immediately after

Short-term effects:
- **Huge integration costs** regarding the **rebranding of the company**, which **required shop re-fits** as well as **a new internet service**
  - **Therefore there were some large costs incurred initially**
- As well as this there **were redundancy costs**, as **the overlap had to be removed** between the businesses

Long-term effects:
- Much **higher profitability and sales**
  - Ability to **continue to grow considerably** over the coming years
- They **were able to remain much more competitive** within the market that **is yet to slow** in growth. The **market has continued to grow very quickly**
  - Therefore with the **record profits announced** it has shown that the merger has been very **successful for TUI and First Choice**

References:

http://www.guardian.co.uk/business/2007/mar/19/travel.travelnews

http://news.bbc.co.uk/1/hi/business/6720995.stm

http://www.guardian.co.uk/business/2007/mar/20/travel.travelnews

http://www.marketingweek.co.uk/thomson-and-first-choice-owner-reports-record-profit/3032449.article

http://www.travelweekly.co.uk/Articles/2011/10/31/38646/tui+shops+become+thomson+featuring+first+choice+in+8m+rebrand.html

Technological Industry

PopCap and EA

PopCap and EA

Merger Formed in:
- **August 2011**

Merger was created because:
- The **merger** was **created**, to try and **make EA more competitive** against the online brand **Zynga.**
- Not only this, but **EA wanted PopCap** to **increase** its **online market share.**
- As the **market moves** to more **internet gaming** and social network gaming, EA wants to use Popcap to be part of this

EA Paid:
- **$750m**

General Public Response (Any Effects, i.e. Price):
- Immediately after the merger, there were **some reservations** about the merger
  - **Consumers worried** that the **quality** of the games would **fall**
    - Counter-argued by EA that the game quality would continue
  - **Consumers worried** that **prices** could **rise**
    - Argued that this would not happen by EA

Media Response:
- **Positive response**, claiming that the move will **strengthen EA**
- Allows a **greater expansion** into **newer countries** and could **benefit public**

Employees Response (Any Effects, i.e. Redundancies):
- **Relatively positive response** as it meant that they could **continue to remain innovative**
- EA plans **to keep jobs** and use PopCap to **develop social gaming**
  - Employees **relatively upbeat** about being transferred to EA

Any Government Intervention:
- **No government intervention** into the merger
  - Agreed by competition commissions, as acquisition would not create a monopoly that is larger than its competitors Zynga, so was deemed not anti-competitive

Sales since acquisition:
- **Profits** for EA in 2011 **more than doubled** in the year
  - EA **earned $221 million**, or 66 cents a share, in the three months that ended June 30.
- **Operating revenue increased to $360bn**

Share Price rise or fall:
- **Shares fell when** shareholders were told that EA was moving **towards more digital gaming**
- EA **shares were down 3.52 percent to $23.32**
- Share prices rose
  - However **share price now down to $16.52**

What the merger meant for EA/PopCap:
- Made it **more competitive** against **its main competitor Zynga**
  - ○ Although **they did not intend** to **remove competition** of Zynga, they did want to become much more competitive against the business
- **Higher innovation** as the business included **a similar market** but a **PopCap focussed** much more on the social market with games such as 'Bejewelled' and 'Plants vs. Zombies'

Any Problems within the business:
- So far **no major problems**
  - ○ However EA now looking to close the gap between themselves and Zynga
- **Could cause Activision to buy Zynga**

Short-term effects:
- **Integration costs** of merging the two businesses together
- **Falling share price**, as shareholders 'run scared' of the new move towards digital gaming
- **Costs incurred** from **movement towards digital campaign**

Long-term effects:
- **Greater market share** into the online gaming market
- **Greater market share for EA** into the **social gaming** market
  - ○ Therefore greater sales due to the awareness of EA
- **Likely greater long term profits**

References:

http://www.telegraph.co.uk/finance/newsbysector/mediatechnologyandtelecoms/digital-media/8633864/Electronic-Arts-buys-PopCap-in-1.3bn-deal.html

http://news.cnet.com/8301-13506_3-20078900-17/ea-acquires-popcap-games-for-digital-push/

http://kotaku.com/5849066/how-popcap-acquired-ea

http://venturebeat.com/2011/07/12/ea-popcap-acquire-750m/

http://www.ingame.msnbc.msn.com/technology/ingame/will-popcaps-sale-hurt-its-games-122243

http://en.wikipedia.org/wiki/Electronic_Arts

http://dealbook.nytimes.com/2011/07/12/in-popcap-deal-electronic-arts-has-its-eyes-on-zynga/

E-bay and PayPal

E-bay and PayPal

Merger Formed in:
- **July 2002**

Merger was created because:
- **50% of users** at e-bay decided to **use PayPal** as their **preferred method** of purchase
  - Therefore the merger would **benefit e-bay** as a form of **forward integration**
- Would continue to **operate as independent brands**
- Aimed to **compete** with **other electronic payments**
  - Hoped that by **purchasing transaction costs** would **fall**
- **More flexibility** to e-bay

E-bay Paid:
- **$1.5bn**

General Public Response (Any Effects, i.e. Price):
- **Mixed** Response:
  - While **some argue** that it is **good** now they have merged **as payments** are **easier** and much **faster**
  - **Others complain** that it **allows e-bay** to **exploit consumers** further as they **own products** as well as the **payment method**
- However, it is argued that the **ownership by e-bay** has made payments **overall easier**

Media Response:
- **Media gave a positive response** of the merger
  - Claimed it was **'a match made in heaven'**
    - **Allowed consumers** to **benefit more** from the **e-bay website**

Any Government Intervention:
- The **government** has **cleared any issues** over the **merger**
  - The **U.S Department of Justice cleared** the deal and agreed that the **merger** would **not** be **anti-competitive**

Employees Response (Any Effects, i.e. Redundancies):

- As it was **decided** that **PayPal** would **continue** as a **separate business** owned by e-bay,
  - Therefore there were **very few redundancies**
- **Offered employees** a **chance to work** within **different business**
  - This therefore meant that **more job opportunities** were **arising**
    - Therefore **staff were motivated** when the company was bought by e-bay, as it **increased job security** for most employees

Sales since acquisition:
- **Growth** has **beaten estimates** repeatedly **over the past 10 years**
  - **Sales** are **continuing** to **grow**
- The **PayPal offers** have also **increased growth** to more than is estimated, which has meant that the merger has been **very successful** for **both PayPal and E-bay**

Share Price rise or fall:
- Since merger until January 2005, **share price rose steadily**.
  - During recession and issues regarding e-bay, share price fell
- However, **after merger** share price **rose from $15.15 to $58.17**.
  - Therefore this shows that **shareholders** believed **merger** was likely to have a **positive** effect

What the merger meant for E-bay/PayPal:
- **Greater ease** to **process transactions** on e-bay
- **Easier use** for consumers
  - Therefore **consumers use e-bay more**
- Possibility to **move into further** markets
  - Therefore greater possibility to **increase profits** in the **long run**

Any Problems within the business:
- **Issues** regarding the **shareholders** who did **not agree** with the **merger**
- **Court filings** regarding the competition issues

Short-term effects:
- **Difficulty to integrate** into **other markets**
  - Cost of **integration**
- Although running as separate businesses, **still had to integrate** some parts of the business that caused some **costs**

Long-term effects:
- **Greater customer service**
- **Larger markets** and **growth** into markets
  - **Greater** long term **profitability**
- **Greater investment** from **shareholders** as share **price rises**

References:

http://news.cnet.com/2100-1017-941964.html

http://www.technewsworld.com/story/18496.html

http://en.wikipedia.org/wiki/PayPal

http://ncws.cnet.com/eBay-PayPal-deal-clears-federal-scrutiny/2100-1017_3-954551.html

http://www.bloomberg.com/news/2012-01-18/ebay-revenue-beats-estimates-on-paypal.html

http://www.pbleepd.com/business/top-10-business-mergersacquisitions-of-the-decade-part-2/

http://www.computeruser.com/articles/banking-on-the-ebay/paypal-merger.html

Disney and Pixar

Disney and Pixar

Merger Formed in:
- **January 2006**

Merger was created because:
- It was believed that the **two could create films** together
  - ○ **As Disney** was aimed **towards children**, a merger with Pixar and the cartoons would make it more possible to **create successful** films
- Disney wanted to **remove part of its competition** by buying Pixar

Disney Paid:
- **$7.4 billion**

General Public Response (Any Effects, i.e. Price):
- At first the public felt that by **moving away from the current Pixar**, it could have **crippling effects** on the business
  - ○ However since **blockbuster films** have continued to be **successful**, the general public have **welcomed the merger** with **open arms**

Media Response:
- It was **assumed** that the merger would **'play out like most'** and either **Pixar** would be **unable** to work with **Disney** or **Disney** would **force the democratic culture** of **Pixar** into the **ground**
  - ○ Therefore the **media** was **sceptical** of the merger
- The **price paid** for Pixar was also **questioned**, as it was believed that Disney paid far **too much** for the company

Any Government Intervention:
- **No government intervention** by the scheme, and it was **agreed by the US Competition commission** as not being anti-competitive

Employees Response (Any Effects, i.e. Redundancies):
- **Employees generally had a positive view** of the acquisition, due to the **promises** that were made to them by **Robert Iger**
  - ○ Promises of particular **job bonuses**, as well as the promise to keep **contracts the same** meant that staff at Pixar were **warming of Disney**
- As claimed by an employee of Pixar, **'We've never had to look back at the list of promises from Disney, because they've always given all of them to us'**
  - ○ Shows therefore that **Iger** made **plans** to make the **merger work**, and was **experienced enough** to make it a success

Sales since acquisition:
- Through films such as 'Cars' and 'Wall-E' it has been **clear** that the **merger** has been considerably **successful**
  - ○ **'Cars' brought billions** in revenue to **Disney**, and the company continues to perform well under the new business
- Therefore the **merger has meant** that **sales** have continued to **rise** since the acquisition by Disney.
  - ○ Merger has meant that the **business remains successful** and is continuing to grow further

Share Price rise or fall:
- **Disney's stock has climbed 28 percent** since its 52-week low on Jan
- **Investor confidence** in the merger
  - ○ Investors believe that **Pixar's cartoons** can be used to **protect** the company **against** the **recession** and therefore confidence in the business is high
- Disney's **share price** has **continued** to **outperform** those of its **competitors**

What the merger meant for Disney/Pixar:
- Disney has **wiped out** part of its **competition**, by buying **Pixar**
  - ○ Pixar and Disney, both who produce films have been able to team up and create films such as 'Wall-E'
    - ▪ Very **successful for both businesses**, with the two going **'hand in hand'**

Any Problems within the business:
- **Considerable corporate culture clashes** between **Steve Jobs**, CEO of Pixar, and **Michael Eisner**, CEO of Disney
  - ○ **Trust** was a serious issue for the two, as they were unable to trust one another, and therefore **tensions arose** between the two
- However, when **Robert Iger** became CEO of Disney, **talks resumed**, and the two were **able to work much more strongly** with one another
  - ○ **Robert Iger** was **experienced** in both **failed**, and **successful mergers** and therefore was able to **keep employees at Pixar** happy and did not force their hands with new contracts

Short-term effects:
- **Some integration issues**, as well as the **corporate clashes** between two CEO's
  - ○ Some issues with the **new employees contracts** and promise to **keep them the same**

Long-term effects:
- **Much higher profitability** and ability to create **huge success films**
  - ○ **Huge returns for Disney**, meaning that the business has continued to grow
- **Removal of competition** also gave Disney a **higher market share** within the film industry **against its other competitors** such as **Warner Brothers**

References:

http://money.cnn.com/2006/01/24/news/companies/disney_pixar_deal/

http://www.cartoonbrew.com/disney/disney-pixar-mergertwo-years-later.html

http://www.nytimes.com/2008/06/01/business/media/01pixar.html?_r=2&oref=login&partner=rssnyt&emc=rss&pagewanted=all

http://www.scpr.org/news/2011/01/24/23248/disney-pixar-merger-5-years-old-today/

http://www.time.com/time/business/article/0,8599,1150674,00.html

http://en.wikipedia.org/wiki/Pixar

AOL and Time Warner

AOL and Time Warner

Merger Formed in:
- **January 2000**

Merger was created because:
- Would **hope to make two companies media powerhouse**
  - AOL was one of the **first large internet providers**
  - **Time Warner had experience in film and video**
    - This was very beneficial to AOL
- Would **strengthen AOL** against new competitors

AOL Paid:
- **$164bn**
  - **Merger** was **valued at $350bn** making the two a media powerhouse

General Public Response (Any Effects, i.e. Price):
- **Excited** for the 'new world' within the internet due to acquisition
  - Thought it would be a **complete success** and would mean new ways of interaction for them on the internet
- Therefore felt that the **merger would be good**, as it would create **huge media opportunity**

Media Response:
- **Mixed response**
  - In some, it was regarded as a way of **increasing the ability** to therefore allow **media** to be **transmitted across internet**
    - Therefore **newspapers would benefit**
  - However some argued that it would **not be a good idea** due to the fact that they had **very different corporate cultures**

Any Government Intervention:
- Although the **merger made them the largest media company**, they did **not face intervention** by the competition commissions, and the **merger was agreed**
  - Deemed not anti-competitive due to the **lack of competition** within the market
    - Therefore were **not forcing competitors out** of the market

Employees Response (Any Effects, i.e. Redundancies):
- **Executives of the company** very **against merger**
  - Considered it to be a **'foolish idea'** and a **'bad move'**
- Therefore they were **strongly opposed** to the idea
  - Later **countless job losses** that also **tore apart the merger**
    - **No motivation and severe job security problems**

Sales since acquisition:
- **Forecasts were not met**, and sales began to **fall considerably**
  - **$99bn loss after the first year** of trading
- Sales **continued to fall** until demerger in 2009
- Therefore the **merger was a failure** in these terms, as sales fell
  - **Overall success also failed due to lack of sales**

Share Price rise or fall:
- As **problems began to arise** share price fell considerably
  - Largest shareholder, one of **the biggest losers of all time**, losing around **$8bn**
- Share price continued to fall until the eventual demerger that occurred in 2009

What the merger meant for AOL/Time Warner:
- **AOL-Time Warner** became the **largest media company** in the world
  - o Therefore they had a **huge market share** and **dominant market powers**
- However the **execution of the merger was a disaster**, and eventually to a large extent, **led** to the **failure** and **hence demerger** of the business
  - o Therefore the **merger should have meant huge profitability**
    - However **executive managers** did **not like** the deal, and therefore it was **executed poorly**

Any Problems within the business:
- **Signs of corporate culture clash** immediately after merger
  - o **'Both sides seemed to hate one another'**
- Due to corporate culture **clashes stock crashed** and the business began to fail with the merger beginning to move towards a close

Short-term effects:
- **Uncertainty by executives** within each company
  - o Were not asked about merger and **merger was agreed behind their backs**
- Therefore the **uncertainty** meant that there were culture clashes
  - o There **were also redundancy costs** and **integration costs**

Long-term effects:
- Corporate **culture clashes** as well as problems within integration
  - o Meant that large redundancies were made
- **Profitability fell** as sales begin to fall significantly meaning that investors saw **share price fall** and therefore the **overall success of the business was being impeded** upon
- Overall led to a **de-merger** and **failure for both businesses**

References:

http://www.telegraph.co.uk/finance/newsbysector/mediatechnologyandtelecoms/media/8031227/A OL-merger-was-the-biggest-mistake-in-corporate-history-believes-Time-Warner-chief-Jeff-Bewkes.html

http://www.nytimes.com/2010/01/11/business/media/11merger.html?pagewanted=all

http://news.cnet.com/2100-1023-235400.html

http://www.wired.com/techbiz/media/news/2000/01/33531

http://en.wikipedia.org/wiki/Time_Warner

http://www.marketplace.org/topics/business/why-time-warner-aol-merger-failed

Amazon and Zappos

Amazon and Zappos

Merger Formed in:
- **December 2009**

Merger was created because:
- To **partly remove** the **competition** of growing Zappos
  - Also argued that some of the **shareholders** were **seeking 'greater liquidity'**
- Therefore **sought greater profits** through the acquired company and combined sales while at the same time **removing some competition** by moving them all under the same name

Amazon Paid:
- **$928m**

General Public Response (Any Effects, i.e. Price):
- **Amazon** very **focussed** on **customers**
  - **Therefore** public was **happy about merger** as it would mean **Zappos** would follow same **route**
- Therefore the **aim to focus on customers** meant public **thought that the merger** was **surprising but beneficial** for **them**

Media Response:
- Some worry about whether it is possible for Zappos' corporate structure to work underneath the Amazon structure
  - However also comment that Zappos' corporate culture has had some effect on the Amazon culture, and therefore may be beneficial to them

Any Government Intervention:
- There was no government intervention, and the sale was made successful in the Autumn of 2009
  - Amazon successfully purchased Zappos without any problems occurring due to the competition commissions on a local or international level

Employees Response (Any Effects, i.e. Redundancies):
- Positive as they move towards a very successful business
  - No intention to cut staff, as there is the intention to remain separate companies
- Amazon seeks to make Zappos as successful as Amazon under the Amazon brand
  - Therefore employees are excited about the acquisition
- Only change is the shareholders

Sales since acquisition:
- Sales have continued to grow since acquisition
  - The brand saw sales growth of 21%
- Zappos has also seen an annual revenue of around $1bn in 2010, which shows the two are continuing to work well, even under the same business

Share Price rise or fall:
- Share price immediately after the announcement of the merger were slightly down for Amazon, less than 1%
  - However Amazon shares have continued to steadily grow since merger, from 128 per share up to 195 per share to date
    - Therefore the merger has allowed for considerable share growth for Amazon

What the merger meant for Amazon/Zappos:
- The merger allowed Zappos to continue to grow with investment from its current investors, as well as innovation from Amazon
  - They were able to continue to operate as a separate non-integrated brand
- Amazon could expect to gain higher profits as well as higher sales
  - Could also have higher market share as was effectively buying the market share

Any Problems within the business:
- There was some concern about corporate culture
  - However this has been very small, and the two have continued to run successfully together
- There was also some problem as they are running as separate business regarding the postage costs and the profit margins on the Zappos products
  - This was quickly resolved by Amazon

Short-term effects:
- Increased publicity from the merger
  - Could be some issues with shareholders, as can be seen by the fall in share price for Amazon
- Takes time to adjust to new Amazon system for Zappos, so productivity may fall by a small amount

Long-term effects:
- Higher market share and profitability for Amazon
  - Continued growth for Zappos, and ability to continue to gain more customers from the customers that use Amazon, and vice versa for Amazon and Zappos customers
- Greater customer service, as well as productivity due to overlap between two brands

References:

http://www.techdirt.com/articles/20090722/1406505622.shtml

http://news.cnet.com/8301-1023_3-10293262-93.html

http://techcrunch.com/2009/07/22/amazon-buys-zappos/

http://paidcontent.org/article/419-breaking-amazon-buying-out-zappos.com-for-807-million-in-stock/

http://uk.finance.yahoo.com/echarts?s=AMZN#symbol=amzn;range=1d;compare=;indicator=volume;charttype=area;crosshair=on;ohlcvalues=0;logscale=off;source=undefined;

http://www.zdnet.com/blog/btl/5-looming-questions-about-the-amazon-zappos-deal/21591

Pharmaceutical

Industry

Glaxo Wellcome and SmithKline Beecham

Glaxo Wellcome and SmithKline Beecham

Merger Formed in:
- **January 2000**

Merger was created because:
- Would make **Glaxo-SmithKline the largest pharmaceutical company** in the world
  - Gives them much **greater market share** and ability to **increase innovation**

Valuation:
- **£114bn**

General Public Response (Any Effects, i.e. Price):
- As **Glaxo-SmithKline** became **the largest pharmaceutical** firm, **lower costs** were expected
  - Some **concerns** it would try to **operate as a monopoly** due to its size and market **power**
- Mixed reaction **regarding competition**
  - Argued against by other companies such as Pfizer

Media Response:
- **Sceptical** due to the past of Glaxo Wellcome and SmithKline Beecham
  - **2nd time** that there has been a **proposition** to **merge** and therefore were not sure whether this one was any more likely
- Used to be **fierce competitors** so there was no certainty that this merger would be successful due to **culture clashes**

Any Government Intervention:
- After **first** proposition to merge, the **government prevented** it
  - This was due to **competition issues**
- However as other pharmaceutical companies merged, and the market became more competitive and more like an oligopoly, the **merger was agreed**

Employees Response (Any Effects, i.e. Redundancies):
- Due to **inevitable job losses**, staff became **demotivated**
  - Due to both **lack of job security**, and poor motivation
- However, those that remained became employees of the largest pharmaceutical company in the world
  - Therefore gives them a **wide reaching number** of job **opportunities**

Sales since acquisition:
- Sales since the acquisition have **continued to grow**
  - Glaxo-SmithKline have managed to gain **some patents** giving them first mover **advantage** over **generic drug companies**
- Therefore the merger has led to **more innovation and higher profits**

Share Price rise or fall:
- Share price has remained **steady** since merger, however before merger the share price did fall by a small amount and did rise after.
  - **Currently sits at 1,430 per share**

What the merger meant for Glaxo Wellcome/SmithKline Beecham:
- **Held 7%** of the global pharmaceutical industry
  - ○ Meant that the industry was able to **operate in London**, while **manufacturing** in the **U.S**
    - ▪ **Gave Glaxo-SmithKline wider markets**

Any Problems within the business:
- Some **law suits** against the new company were raised
  - ○ **Competition issues regular**, however no major issues regarding the merger between the two firms, and since this sales and size have both increased

Short-term effects:
- **Cost of integration**
- **Job Losses**
  - ○ Therefore **redundancy costs**, as well as a fall in **staff morale**
    - ▪ Possible **production issues**

Long-term effects:
- Much **larger economies of scale**
  - ○ This is due to the **innovation between** the two companies
    - ▪ Form of **horizontal integration** and therefore they were **simply merging** the **two companies** producing very similar goods
- **Sharing of knowledge** giving them **better productivity**
  - ○ **Lower unit cost**

References:

http://www.wsws.org/articles/2000/jan2000/glax-j22.shtml

http://crossborder.practicallaw.com/2-101-4509

http://news.bbc.co.uk/1/hi/business/606479.stm

http://news.bbc.co.uk/1/hi/business/606752.stm

http://news.bbc.co.uk/1/hi/business/606830.stm

http://www.thepharmaletter.com/file/72975/glaxo-wellcome-smithkline-beecham-merger-updated-story.html

Pfizer and Pharmacia

Pfizer and Pharmacia

Merger Formed in:
- **March 2003**

Merger was created because:
- To **compete against other growing pharmaceutical companies** such as Glaxo Wellcome and SmithKline Beecham
  - Therefore **many** pharmaceutical companies were **following the same path** of mergers and **external growth** to **increase competition**
    - Therefore they had to merge to some extent, **to remain competitive**

Pfizer Paid:
- **$60bn**

General Public Response (Any Effects, i.e. Price):
- **General public views it as quite positive**, as it makes it one of the **largest pharmaceutical companies**, which therefore could reduce costs
  - Could therefore **benefit general public** due to **economies of scale reducing the costs** of production that could be passed on to consumers

Media Response:
- The **media viewed it as unsurprising**, due to the number of companies within the industry that were following the same path
  - Therefore they were **not particularly surprised** when the merger was proposed
    - However they **were surprised at the time it took** for the **Competition Commissions** to agree with the merger
- This is **considering that GSK** also went through a merger and did not face delays by competition

Any Government Intervention:
- When the **merger was first proposed** it was **halted by the ECC**
  - The **ECC requested further information** from both companies before taking the next steps before agreeing the merger
  - The **USCC has also requested further information from Pfizer** before giving the go ahead

Employees Response (Any Effects, i.e. Redundancies):
- There were **no real complaints** as Pfizer was already one of the largest suppliers of pharmaceuticals in the world
  - Therefore the **move to merge the two together** was not a particular surprise
    - There was **some concern about large job cuts**, however it was expected that most cuts would come due to overlap

Sales since acquisition:
- **Sales have continued to grow** with Pfizer's **Viagra**, **Zoloft** and other products, mixed with Pharmacia's **Nicorette** and **Celebrex**
  - Therefore the merger has allowed the **two businesses combine sales** which has therefore seen growing sales
    - However as **patents begin to expire, sales** may begin **to fall**

Share Price rise or fall:
- After the **announcement** of the **merger**, both **businesses** and their **shareholders** saw **different responses**
  - While **Pharmacia shares rose $6.66 to $39.25 per share**
    - **Pfizer shares fell more than 10% to $28.78** per share
- Shares **now for Pfizer are $22.49**

What the merger meant for Pfizer/Pharmacia:
- It **allowed them to integrate** the **innovation costs**, and **therefore** while **not only becoming** innovative, they could **save some research costs**, as the two would be operating together
  - They could **also increase the market share** and become **further profitable**
  - They had a **large number** of products that were **patented** and by joining together this could be **reserved**

Any Problems within the business:
- Some **problems regarding the integration** of the business
  - It is almost **impossible for a merger to occur without some issues**
- However it was a **smooth merger in general**, and **Pfizer continues to be one of the largest** pharmaceutical companies

Short-term effects:
- There were **integration costs**
  - Costs in **combining innovation** as well as **redundancy costs**
    - They were **receiving some bad publicity** due to their **patents** and they were also beginning to **fall behind competition** for a short time **due to integration**

Long-term effects:
- Much **higher innovation** abilities, as well as **profitability and sales**
  - A much **higher market share** could be achieved as well as the ability to **reduce** the **time to produce products**, due to the factories that can be used by the new company as the two have integrated together
- Therefore they would be much **more competitive**, to some extent **widening the gap** between **their competitors**

References:

http://news.bbc.co.uk/1/hi/business/2129300.stm

http://www.inpharm.com/news/eu-suspends-pfizerpharmacia-merger-review

http://www.cbc.ca/news/business/story/2002/07/15/pfizer_020715.html

http://uk.finance.yahoo.com/q?s=PFE

http://www.chelationtherapyonline.com/technical/p39.htm

http://en.wikipedia.org/wiki/Pfizer

Financial Industry

JPMorgan Chase and Bank One Corporation

J. P. Morgan Chase and Bank One Corporation

Merger Formed in:
- **June 2004**

Merger was created because:
- Would make the merged company the **second largest bank** behind Citigroup
  - Therefore it would have much **greater market share**
- Would gain a **strong retail** and **credit balance** from **Bank One Corporation**

J. P. Morgan Chase Paid:
- **$58bn**

General Public Response (Any Effects, i.e. Price):
- **Positive response**, as customers benefit from the merger
  - **Better services** from the merger of the new bank
- Possible **better credit** from the **new business**

Media Response:
- Very **positive** of the merger
  - Claimed it as having **'a real logic'**
- Viewed that the **two businesses** would go **hand in hand** and be very **successful**

Any Government Intervention:
- **Passed** stress **tests** by the **U.S Financial Department**
- Also **passed** the tests by the **Competition Commissions**

Employees Response (Any Effects, i.e. Redundancies):
- **Creation of jobs**
  - Therefore **employees** were **in agreement** about the merger
- Allowed **integration between different markets** within the financial markets
  - Therefore employees had a **greater choice** and **ability of movement**

Sales since acquisition:
- **Growing sales** continuing since the **merger** between the two businesses. J. P. Morgan Chase has continued to **see rising profits** during the financial years
  - However **profits did fall** under **the global credit crisis** that **affected all financial sectors**

Share Price rise or fall:
- **Since merger** share price rose from **$34.17** per share **to $51.83** per share which showed that **shareholders** were **confident** about the merger
  - However during the global crisis in **2009 share price fell to $25.51**, however all financial sectors globally but especially in America were effected by the banking crisis

What the merger meant for J. P. Morgan Chase/Bank One Corporation:
- There was **integration between the two firms** giving them **huge market share**
  - ○ Made them **2nd largest bank in America**
- Meant that they were **appealing to a much wider** market
  - ○ Although both banks, **one was more investment** while **one was more based on retail** so they fitted well as allowed an **integration** between **investment** and **retail** banking
- Made them much **more competitive** against firms such as Citigroup

Any Problems within the business:
- Some **difficulties** regarding **competition**
  - ○ This **was later cleared** however

Short-term effects:
- **Integration costs** between the two businesses
  - ○ Costs due to **some redundancies**
- Cost to **integrate the different** parts of the business as there was **full integration**

Long-term effects:
- Much **higher profitability**
  - ○ Due to **wider markets**, it allowed for more **consumers to use J. P. Morgan Chase**
- Much **greater market share**
- Possible **greater economies of scale**

References:

http://money.cnn.com/2004/01/14/news/deals/jpmorgan_bankone/

http://www.jpmorganchase.com/corporate/About-JPMC/jpmorgan-history.htm
http://banking.about.com/od/bankaccountreview1/a/JPMorgan-Chase-Bank-Review-History.htm

http://topics.nytimes.com/top/news/business/companies/morgan_j_p_chase_and_company/index.html

http://findassignment.blogspot.co.uk/2008/05/jp-morgan-chase-and-bank-one-merger.html

http://uk.finance.yahoo.com/echarts?s=JPM#symbol=jpm;range=my;compare=;Indlcator=volume,charttype=area;crosshair=on;ohlcvalues=0;logscale=off;source=undefined;

http://www.jpmorganchase.com/corporate/About-JPMC/document/shorthistory.pdf

JPMorgan and Chase Manhattan

JPMorgan and Chase Manhattan

Merger Formed in:
- **January 2001**

Merger was created because:
- Would **allow them to increase investment banking** market
  - As well as **keeping the commercial banking sector**
- Therefore they would **become more competitive against banks** such **as Citigroup**
- Many other **investment and commercial banks** are following the **same trend**
  - Therefore **JPMorgan Chase** was established to **strengthen their position**

Chase Manhattan Paid:
- Valuation of **$28.6bn for the merger**
  - Making them **3rd largest bank**

General Public Response (Any Effects, i.e. Price):
- **Very little was known** about this merger by the public, and therefore they did not have a large amount to say about the merger
  - The **merger was argued as anti-competitive by some**, as it would give them abusive **market powers**, however these views soon changed when **JPMorgan Chase** was able to **offer** more **effective services to consumers**

Media Response:
- The media portrayed it as **'just another merger'** as the **financial market** was **involved** in a **number of mergers**, including **Bank of America and Merrill Lynch** as well as other financial banks
  - Therefore they did **not particularly see the deal** as **surprising**
- However they **did feel that it could be good for both JPMorgan and Chase Manhattan**, and allow them to **remain competitive within Wall Street**

Any Government Intervention:
- **FED approved the merger** without making any sacrifices to either business
  - Therefore the **FED felt that it would not lead to anti-competitive behaviour** by the bank, and it approved the go ahead
- There was **investigation into the merger**, as the two banks were the **3rd and 5th largest US banks**, however the government later felt that there was **no reason to prevent the merger**

Employees Response (Any Effects, i.e. Redundancies):
- Although there were some **unsurprising redundancies**, employees were **generally happy about the merger**. It gave them the ability to **continue to expand as a business**

Sales since acquisition:
- **Continued to remain the 3rd largest bank in America**
  - They have **continued to grow in their investment sector**, and are considered likely to continue to **grow even** during the **damaging credit crunch crisis of 2008**
- However it is **not surprising that equity and therefore profit did fall during** the credit crunch **crisis**
  - The merger has been **relatively successful for JPMorgan Chase** and its continued growth

Share Price rise or fall:
- **Immediately after** the announcement of the merger, **share price** for both Chase Manhattan and JPMorgan **fell**
  - ○ **Chase Manhattan** saw shares **fall $2.13 to $50.69 per share**
  - ○ **JPMorgan** saw shares fall **$4.19 to £181.25**
    - ▪ Therefore there was **some suspicion about the acquisition** by Chase Manhattan
- However now the **share price for JPMorgan Chase has continued to grow**, with the merger proving to be a considerable success

What the merger meant for JPMorgan/Chase Manhattan:
- **The merger allowed JPMorgan Chase** to remain **competitive against other** banks within the US
  - ○ The **investment bank sector** for the business also **grew considerably**
- Therefore it was a **merger that allowed the bank to continue** to grow within an increasingly competitive market

Any Problems within the business:
- **Problems with integration short term**, as well as the **redundancies made** with the cost savings from **overlap of $1.5bn**

Short-term effects:
- **Integration costs of $2.8bn** to **combine** the two companies **and remove overlap**
- **Cost savings of $1.5bn** as staff were **removed due to overlap**
  - ○ Time to **integrate the two cultures together**

Long-term effects:
- Allowed the **business to continue to grow** at a considerable rate, even **during recession**
  - ○ **Still one of the largest banks** in the world and in the US
- Has allowed **investment banking to increase** and become more **competitive against banks** such as **Citigroup**
- Therefore it has **proved to make the bank more profitable** and more **successful**

References:

http://money.cnn.com/2000/09/13/deals/chase_morgan/

http://articles.latimes.com/2000/dec/12/business/fi-64339

http://en.wikipedia.org/wiki/JPMorgan_Chase

http://finance.mapsofworld.com/merger-acquisition/company/chase-manhattan-jp-morgan.html

http://abcnews.go.com/Business/story?id=89367&page=1#.T3G8N5j3DoA

http://www.saflii.org/za/cases/ZACT/2000/52.html

Bank of America and Merrill Lynch

Bank of America and Merrill Lynch

Merger Formed in:
- **September 2008**

Merger was created because:
- Would **combine commercial bank with investment bank**
  - Therefore both would be able to **combine into new markets allowing** them to **grow** within **different markets towards different consumers**
- They would be able to **increase profitability through merging** to create one larger bank which is **more competitive**

Bank of America Paid:
- **$50bn**

General Public Response (Any Effects, i.e. Price):
- **General public did not have much say** before the merger
  - However **NY then followed by filing civil breach of law** and suing **BOA for fraud**

Media Response:
- The **media thought it was a terrible idea** after the merger was **agreed within 48 hours**
  - Many other **mergers have failed the same way**
    - Therefore the **media argued it was a very poor decision** to make, due to the **corporate cultures** that clash between investment and commercial banking
- Therefore they **were not surprised** when BOA almost **immediately began to fail** after the merger

Any Government Intervention:
- The **government did not intervene**, as it did not give them a huge advantage over their competitors
  - They **approved the merger,** but only weeks after it was approved, it was considered to be **failing**, and led to a **de-merger not long after**
- Therefore the **merger was deemed a complete failure**, one that the **CEO of BOA still regrets to this day**
  - Also cost the **US Reserve huge bailout funds** to prevent BOA from falling the same way as Lehman Brothers

Employees Response (Any Effects, i.e. Redundancies):
- A **large number of employees of BOA and Merrill Lynch left**, including the **CEO of BOA** and the **CEO of Merrill Lynch**
  - The **president of BOA** also had **to leave due to the issues** that caused the failure of the **merger**
- Therefore employees were **leaving** as well as being made **redundant** very quickly, destroying **job security and satisfaction**, as more and more employees became more and more stressed

Sales since acquisition:
- The **disaster of BOA** and Merrill Lynch was known **22 days after the merger** was carried out
  - There was the need to **borrow $118bn** from government reserves, which shows that **the two did not manage to increase sales at all**
- **Sales fell considerably** and the merger was **deemed a compete failure**

Share Price rise or fall:
- **Share price fell 78% within months** of the merger for Bank of America, showing that the merger was a **total disaster**
  - Led to **investors running and moving away from BOA** which made it even more difficult for BOA to revive its share price
- It was **argued that BOA paid far too much for Merrill** Lynch which is what caused such disastrous falls in share price
  - Merrill Lynch was **trading at $17** per share but **BOA bought them for $29** per share

What the merger meant for Bank of America/Merrill Lynch:
- The **failure in the merger meant that sales fell, investment fell** and **reputation plummeted**
  - **The merger left BOA** in a financially **unstable position**, and they were being **protected by the American government from entirely failing**
- Therefore the **merger destroyed share price, reputation** and **publicity** for BOA and Merrill Lynch only a month after the merger had been fully carried out

Any Problems within the business:
- Huge **corporate culture clashes** between Merrill Lynch and BOA that made it impossible for them to fully integrate
  - The two businesses were **unable to continue to operate together**
- The bank was **unable to complete integration**
- **Eventually led to a demerger of the two**

Short-term effects:
- There were **huge integration costs**
  - There were costs involved in **making some staff redundant**
- **Huge amounts were borrowed** from the **Federal Reserve**
- **Shortly after led to de-merger** due to corporate culture clashes between two banks

Long-term effects:
- **Market share for BOA fell considerably** and it has still been **unable to gain the market share** that it once had
  - Therefore **reputation** as well as profits have caused the bank to **lose considerable market capitalization**
- This shows therefore that the **merger did to a large extent destroy** the **prospects of the bank and overall damaged** the banking **sector as a whole**

References:

http://blogs.wsj.com/deals/2009/01/22/bank-of-america-merrill-lynch-a-50-billion-deal-from-hell/

http://www.csmonitor.com/USA/2010/0204/New-York-sues-Bank-of-America-over-Merrill-Lynch-merger

http://www.nytimes.com/2009/02/08/business/08split.html?pagewanted=all

http://www.washingtonpost.com/wp-dyn/content/article/2008/09/14/AR2008091401468.html

http://en.wikipedia.org/wiki/Merrill_Lynch

HSBC and Household International

HSBC and Household International

Merger Formed in:
- March 2003

Merger was created because:
- HSBC wanted to **become part of the US housing market**
  - **US housing market was booming**
  - **Household International** was a **large sub-prime mortgage lender**
- Therefore **HSBC acquired Household International** to try and become **part of the housing market** due to the size of Household International
  - However **Household International** had a **disreputable past**

HSBC Paid:
- **$14.2bn**

General Public Response (Any Effects, i.e. Price):
- **General public** in the US benefitted it as they were able to **effectively exploit the bank,** by **taking out loans** on things they **wished to buy and later defaulted**
  - Therefore **low-income US citizens** welcomed the merger as they would **benefit**
- However **UK citizens did not welcome it so highly,** with a number **criticizing** the deal as **'absurd'**

Media Response:
- The media were **very against the acquisition**
  - They claimed that **Household International** did **not fit** with the **operations of HSBC,** and this **caused damage** to **reputation** and **profitability of HSBC**
- **HSBC was hit by $30bn** loss due to **Household International** which did nothing more than to back up the media's view that it was a poor response and the merger was not researched enough by HSBC

Any Government Intervention:
- There was **not any intervention into the purchase,** as HSBC currently does not operate in the US household market
  - Therefore it would **not be anti-competitive** for HSBC to buy Household International
- There was some investigation into the scheme, however it was later **approved by U.S Financial Department**

Employees Response (Any Effects, i.e. Redundancies):
- Initially it was **welcomed by the staff of both HSBC and Household International**
  - However when HSBC decided that the scheme was working it **shut down the 800 outlets** for Household International
    - This meant **large numbers of redundancies** and these did cause some issues within the U.S
- However **a large number of people were being made redundant** in the **financial markets** due to the **credit crisis**

Sales since acquisition:
- **Sales continued to rise** until the scheme eventually failed and led to the **huge debts** that HSBC were welcomed with. Therefore **sales were short term**

Share Price rise or fall:
- **Share price initially** before the **merger fell**
  - It did **begin to improve, however** this improvement was **very short term**, and share price fell for **Household International** when the **citizens of the mortgages defaulted on their loans**
- Therefore share price did **once again fall**
  - However for **HSBC this has improved** and share price is currently at **563.18 per share**
    - It did **understandably fall** during the recession as all **banks' share price did**

What the merger meant for HSBC/Household International:
- **Household International** had **'piggyback loans'**
  - Therefore there was **high interest** which is what meant that **HSBC could benefit**
- However as **low income citizens** defaulted on loans, **more problems arose**
- Should have **allowed HSBC to increase profitability**, and expand into **new markets**
  - However HSBC chose a **weak business** with **poor reputation**

Any Problems within the business:
- These **sub-prime mortgage**s led to **high debt for HSBC**, as US citizens were defaulting on loans, **leaving the debt to HSBC**
  - Therefore **cash flow became restricted**
  - **Reputation was also damaged,** as profitability was damaged by Household

Short-term effects:
- **Integration costs**
  - However foot into the door of US housing market
- Therefore **HSBC profitability did increase** by a small amount in the short term

Long-term effects:
- The **merger very quickly ended**, as it was these **sub-prime mortgages that** caused the credit crunch
  - **Companies were beginning to file for redundancy** and HSBC therefore **closed Household International**
- Therefore it **carried the debt of Household** International which is what sparked the fist part of the credit crunch
- **Very poor long term effects** including **high debt**, and **poor reputation**

References:

http://www.nytimes.com/2009/03/06/business/economy/06norris.html?pagewanted=all

http://www.pbleepd.com/business/top-10-business-mergersacquisitions-of-the-decade-part-2/

http://www.efinancialnews.com/story/2003-01-06/deal-profile-hsbc-tackles-the-us

http://www.hsbc.com/1/2/newsroom/news/2003/hsbc-completes-the-acquisition-of-household

http://www.google.co.uk/finance?client=ob&q=LON:HSBA

http://www.forbes.com/2002/11/14/cx_pm_1114hsbc.html

Petroleum Industry

Exxon and Mobil

Exxon and Mobil

Merger Formed in:
- **November 1999**

Merger was created because:
- It would give them **greater efficiency** and **lower transport costs**
- Would also **increase market share**
  - As they are the 1st largest and 2nd largest, the merger would make them **considerably larger**
- Would make them the **3rd largest company in the world**

Exxon Paid:
- **$81bn**

General Public Response (Any Effects, i.e. Price):
- **General public** initially were **worried** that the merger could lead to **dominant market powers**
  - Other oil companies **(competitors)** also **argued the same**
- Therefore **initially** they were **against the merger**
  - However **since the merger**, the general public seem **happy** about the merger as it has made it **possible** to **reduce oil prices** or **hold them steady**, due to **exploration**

Media Response:
- **Media argued** that the two **companies would fit well** together under the new merger
  - The **two would work together** as they could **combine exploration** while continuing to **grow with its stations**
- The **media argued** that it would **benefit the customers** with the merger of the two, and therefore they agreed with the merger

Any Government Intervention:
- **The FTC approved** the merger after a promise to **sell 2,431 stations**
  - Thus the **FTC did intervene** in this instance, to **prevent anti-competitive** behaviour by **Exxon and Mobil**
- However once this was agreed, the merger was set to go ahead

Employees Response (Any Effects, i.e. Redundancies):
- **Plans to cut 9000** (7.3%) jobs to save money
  - Therefore **some disagreement** by the employees of Mobil and Exxon
- The **job cuts meant** that there were **some issues directly after merger**
  - However, the **new merger** did **particularly benefit employees** due to its **size** and **ability for growth**

Sales since acquisition:
- **Sales have continued to grow strongly**
  - **Revenue for 2011** was at **$486bn**
    - Therefore continues to be one of the **largest suppliers** in the world
- ExxonMobil, has continued to **remain highly competitive** with sales continuing to grow, **even** as **oil prices** continue to **rise**

Share Price rise or fall:
- Shareholders were **not particularly happy** about the deal
  - Therefore they were **not happy about the payoff** during the acquisition
- This meant that the **share price also fell considerably** and **de-valued** the **value** of the merger to **around $76bn**
  - **However since** the merger, **share price has grown**, partly due to the **success of the merger**, but **also** due to **rising oil prices**

What the merger meant for Exxon/Mobil:
- The **merger benefitted** not only the **employees and shareholders** but also the **customers**
  - **Savings** on **exploration costs** meant that the **two businesses fitted** one another well
- They would be **even more competitive** against their competitors
  - Thus the **profitability would increase**
  - **Sales** would also **increase**

Any Problems within the business:
- There were **some issues regarding** the staff **redundancies**
  - However these were **brief** and made **little difference** to success of merger
- **Merger overall been a considerably large success**
- The **FTC did prevent some stations** from remaining under ExxonMobil ownership

Short-term effects:
- **Integration costs**
  - However after **the selling of stores**, these were **mostly covered**
- **Lower profitability** as a large number of **stores had to be sold**
  - Therefore the **overall sales and revenue also fell**

Long-term effects:
- **Greater profitability** and **sales**
  - This is due to the **costs being saved on exploration**, as well as savings made on costs of employees
    - **Staff redundancies due to overlap**
- Therefore the **overall profit increased**, as well as the **market share continuing to remain high**
- Overall therefore made them **3rd largest business** and **largest oil producer in the world**
  - **Largest public owned company in US**

References:

http://money.cnn.com/1999/11/30/deals/exxonmobil/

http://money.cnn.com/1998/12/01/deals/exxon/

http://en.wikipedia.org/wiki/ExxonMobil

http://news.bbc.co.uk/1/hi/business/222402.stm

http://www.rasmussen.edu/degrees/business/blog/best-and-worst-corporate-mergers/

http://www.ftc.gov/opa/1999/03/met1.shtm

BP and Amoco

BP and Amoco

Merger Formed in:
- **December 1998**

Merger was created because:
- Recommended by both boards (**Friendly Takeover**)
  - Allows for **greater exploration**
- Can **save costs on production**
  - Both are similar however **BP specialises in exploration** and research while **Amoco specialises in transportation**

BP Paid:
- **$110bn**

General Public Response (Any Effects, i.e. Price):
- While the **reserves and oil supply** was **plentiful** there was likely to be **little effect felt** by the consumer
  - **However as prices rise** due to the oil beginning to become more limited, there may be **some negative views** about the **size** of BP
- Other **oil executives** said that the **merger benefitted** both **BP and Amoco**, and that it was a good approach to take

Media Response:
- Generally a **positive response** to the **merger**.
  - By the merger taking place, it meant that **BP grew in size** and could have a **positive effect** on consumers, particularly in the long run
- Therefore the **media complimented the scheme**

Any Government Intervention:
- After analysis of the merger, it was **agreed in 1998** by the **US Federal Trade Commission**
  - This therefore meant that there was **no government intervention** and the sale could go ahead, meaning the merger could continue
- Although it **gave BP considerable market advantage**, it is a highly concentrated market
  - Deemed **not anti-competitive**

Employees Response (Any Effects, i.e. Redundancies):
- **Expected 6000 job cuts** so there was some **job security** issues
  - Some staff felt **de-motivated** due to this
- Job cuts **necessary** due to the **integration** of the business
  - However **most** at the **research level**
    - Some also in **Cleveland production**

Sales since acquisition:
- **Oil** prices have **continued to soar**, and therefore sales continue to mean **higher profits**
  - As emerging markets grow, BP continues to **grow in size through** further **mergers** and therefore profits continue to rise

Share Price rise or fall:
- **Shares surged 15%** after the news of the merger between BP and Amoco
- There will be **a 60 – 40 split** between the two companies
  - Shares rose to **874.5p per share** after the announcement of the new merger
    - This **was up 101.5p**
- Therefore this shows that shareholders had **confidence in the merger**

What the merger meant for BP/Amoco:
- Greater **ability** to **increase profits**, particularly in the **long run**
- Ability to **remove overlap** between two firms
  - Therefore **cost minimisation**
    - **Porter**
- Greater sales due to **publicity** from merger

Any Problems within the business:
- **Limits on exploration**
- **Competition problems**

Short-term effects:
- **Integration costs** between two businesses
- **Redundancies**
  - Could possibly affect production

Long-term effects:
- **Ability to combine exploration**
  - **Increase innovation** while keeping costs down
- **Greater profitability**
- **Lower unit costs**
  - Due to ability to share transportation and production costs
    - **Amoco specialises in transportation**

References:

http://news.bbc.co.uk/1/hi/149139.stm

http://www.bp.com/liveassets/bp_internet/globalbp/STAGING/global_assets/downloads/A/Amoco_Key_facts_and_highlights.pdf

http://www.bp.com/genericarticle.do?categoryId=2012968&contentId=2001131

http://www.nytimes.com/1998/08/12/business/british-petroleum-is-buying-amoco-in-48.2-billion-deal.html?pagewanted=all&src=pm

Conclusion of Mergers and Acquisitions

Good Mergers:

1. Tata and Jaguar Land Rover
2. Kraft and Cadburys
3. Adidas and Reebok
4. Thompsons and First Choice
5. PopCap and EA
6. E-bay and PayPal
7. Disney and Pixar
8. Amazon and Zappos
9. Glaxo Wellcome and SmithKline Beecham
10. Pfizer and Pharmacia
11. JPMorgan and Bank One Corporation
12. JPMorgan and Chase Manhattan
13. Exxon and Mobil
14. BP and Amoco

Bad Mergers:

1. Daimler and Chrysler
2. Ford and Jaguar Land Rover
3. Co-op and Somerfield
4. L'Oreal and The Body Shop
5. Sears and Kmart
6. Mattel and The Learning Company

Ugly Mergers:

1. Quaker and Snapple
2. AOL and Time Warner
3. Bank of America and Merrill Lynch
4. HSBC and Household International

Overall Summary of Mergers and Acquisitions

Overall therefore, we can come to the conclusion about mergers and acquisitions in general, and what they depend on.

So what do they depend on?

The answer to what they depend on, are a number of factors, including time, research and the corporate culture of the businesses that are intending to merge. Not only this, but the amount of money that is invested into integration as well as a number of other factors also play a significant role on how well the merger or acquisition is likely to succeed.

Therefore a business that puts little or no time into the research stages of an acquisition, much like HSBC and Household International, is likely to have to face huge problems, and a very realistic chance of a de-merger of a sale of the business that they acquired. Another factor that tends to catch businesses out is the speed at which they either merge or acquire one another. If there is a bidding war, then they will try to be the first one out at the other end, with the business they intended to buy. Therefore they may not only have not realised some things about the business that lead to the failure of the merger/acquisition, but they may also pay to much for a business, much like many financial deals have ended in.

Therefore when a business considers a merger or acquisition, it is important that they actually look in detail at how successful the business that they wish to partner with is. If they fail to do this, then they may end up on the list of ugly mergers/acquisitions. If they carry out their research well, and the two businesses are able to integrate successfully, then they are likely to end up on the list of good mergers/acquisitions, such as Tata and JLR or Disney and Pixar (after a few issues). If they simply are unable to remain together, then they are likely to end up on the list of bad mergers/acquisitions.

So how do you go about using these examples in an essay?

One of the most important parts of this book is this page here that follows the list of the examples.

While it is not necessary to read this entire in depth summary of all the different examples that exist, it is advised that you learn 3 good mergers/acquisitions, 3 bad mergers/acquisitions and 3 ugly mergers/acquisitions. By doing this, you are covering all the bases when it comes to writing an essay, whether it may be Business Studies, or Economics.

The most important thing when writing the essay is to not simply include a story about a business. By writing a story, you are likely to receive no credit towards a paragraph within your essay, as it is not directly linked to the essay title. Therefore the most important thing you must be able to do successfully, is extract the important parts of information from the different areas of a business. This is exactly what this book has been designed to help do. While you are unlikely to need all the information about each business described in this book, you are more than likely going to need to know some of the information.

Therefore the most important thing that you can do is learning the different facts and figures for each business, which you can relate to an essay. By doing this, you are effectively able to prevent yourself from going off on a tangent when writing something interesting about an essay. Once again, the MOST important thing that you must do when answering an essay title, is answer the question. Do not wander off in an entirely different direction, which does not validate a paragraph, because you will not receive credit for it.

If you can do this, then you are likely to succeed when adding examples to an essay to strengthen an argument. Remember, evidence is fact, and fact is what strengthens an argument. I hope that after reading this book your mind is filled with good examples, bad examples and ugly examples, and I wish you the best of luck when it comes to taking your exam.

Remember, answer the question, and don't go off on a tangent!

www.ingramcontent.com/pod-product-compliance
Lightning Source LLC
Chambersburg PA
CBHW051324170526
45166CB00002B/676